A FRACTURED LEXICON

VOLUME II

THINGS I FORGOT TO PUT IN VOLUME I

<u>TO YOU</u>
FOR MAKING
VOLUME I
SUCH A SUCCESS

Efstathiadis Group S.A.
Agiou Athanasiou Street,
GR - 145 65 Anixi. Attikis

ISBN 960 226 429 2

© Efstathiadis Group S.A. 1993

Printed and bound in Greece by Efstathiadis Group S.A.

HANDWRITTEN BY:VERNON VAS ELLIOTT
ILLUSTRATED BY " " "

I DO WANT TO EXPRESS
MY THANKS TO THE
THOUSANDS OF PEOPLE
WHO, AFTER THE
PUBLICATION OF VOLUME I
SAID TO ME: "HOW ABOUT
THAT ONE-YOU FORGOT IT"
THUS PROVIDING ME,
VERY QUICKLY, WITH
THE MATERIAL FOR
VOLUME II.
KEEP IT UP. THERE
MAY EVEN BE VOLUME III

CONTENTS

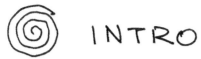 # INTRO

EVEN IN MY WILDEST DREAMS
I NEVER EXPECTED THIS THING TO
GO SO FAR. I NOW FIND MYSELF
SPEAKING GREEK BY TRANSLATING
ENGLISH IDIOMS, AND ENGLISH BY
REVERSING THE PROCESS!!!
IT IS AN ENIGMATIC WAY TO PUT
THINGS, IT MAKES PEOPLE, STOP
THINK & LAUGH ONCE THEY GO
THROUGH THE PROCESS THEMSELVES.
THE SUCCESS OF VOLUME I,
FUELED VOLUME II. THE SMILING,
LAUGHING, AMUSED FACES WHEN
READING VOLUME I, ALSO GIVE
ONE THE MOTIVATION & COURAGE
TO COMPOSE MORE LITTLE BOOKS
LIKE THIS.

I am neither a writer, nor a caricaturist.
I have a hard time with both. I do like
languages though in all their extremes, from
high to low. People are very creative,
regardless of their education with their languages.

Please forgive any liberties I may have
taken in poting this thing together.
As I mentioned in VOLUME I, if you have
any better ideas, or you can do a better job
then write your own book

INSTRUCTIONS

Again I tried desperately to put some order to this thing. I tried going by verb, or making units by meaning but I couldn't. It took away from the spontaneity of it all. If you have any bright ideas please let me know for the next edition, to make it NEW & IMPROVED much like TIDE or COCA COLA.

The guide to pronunciation, such as it was, is not repeated here. Reference must be made to VOLUME I. I just hope you no longer need it.

The format remains the same

1 - Greek idiom
2 - Phonetic pronunciation
3 - Literal translation

4 - EQUIVALENT ENGLISH AMERICAN EXPRESSION OR MEANING

Again there may be an illustration and then may be not. Depends on the images the expression creates and how difficult it is to put them on paper. I tried hiring a caricaturist, a proper one that is but it was too expensive a proposition.

So you are, once more, stuck with mine.

IDIOMS

TON EBAΛE ΣTO MATI

TON ÉVALE STO MÁTEE

HE PUT HIM IN HIS EYE

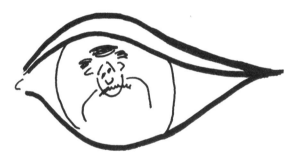

① HE HAS HIS EYE ON HIM
② HE'S GOT IT IN FOR HIM

METPHMENA KOYKIA

METREEMÉNA KOOKIÁ

COUNTED BROAD BEANS

◎ IT'S IN THE BAG

◎ ALL FIXED

ΕΙΝΑΙ ΝΑ ΤΡΕΛΛΑΘΕΙΣ

EENE NA TRELATHÉES

IT IS TO GO CRAZY

◎ IT'S ENOUGH TO DRIVE YOU MAD

A PHRASE VERY FREQUENTLY HEARD
IN AND AROUND PUBLIC AND GOVERNMENT
BUILDINGS, BUT MANY OTHER PLACES AS WELL

ΓΙΑ ΤΑ ΜΑΤΙΑ ΤΟΥ ΚΟΣΜΟΥ

yiá τα μάτια του cósmoo

FOR THE EYES OF THE WORLD

◉ FOR OTHERS TO SEE, BUT OF NO SUBSTANCE

◉ FOR THE SAKE OF APPEARANCES

18

ΑΛΛΑΞΕ ΤΟ ΒΙΟΛΙ ΤΟΥ

ÁLLAKSE TO VIOLEÉ TOO

HE CHANGED HIS VIOLIN

◎ HE CHANGED HIS TUNE

◎ HE SANG ANOTHER TUNE

ΔΕΝ ΕΙΣΑΙ ΜΕ ΤΑ ΚΑΛΑ ΣΟΥ

THEN EÉSE ME TA KALÁ SOO

YOU'RE NOT WITH YOUR GOODS

- YOU'VE TAKEN LEAVE OF YOUR SENSES
- YOU MUST BE CRAZY (INSANE, A NUT)
- ARE YOU IN YOUR RIGHT MIND?
  (clearly implying that one is demented
  or mentally deranged, at least.)

ΦΟΥΡΝΟΣ ΝΑ ΜΗ ΚΑΠΝΙΣΕΙ

FOÓRNOS NA MEE KAPNEÉSEE

AN OVEN   NO TO SMOKE
  (BAKERY)

◎ I COULD CARE LESS

◎ I DON'T GIVE A DARN

BΓHKE AΠ'TA POYXA TOY

vgeéke apta roóha too

HE GOT OUT OF HIS CLOTHES

🌀 HE WAS BOWLED OVER

🌀 HE WAS KNOCKED OFF HIS FEET

🌀 HE WAS FLABBERGASTED

ONOMA KAI MH XΩPIO
ΌNOMA KE MEE HORIÓ
NAME AND NO VILLAGE

⊚ MENTION NO NAME

ΠΙΝΕΙ ΣΑΝ ΣΦΟΥΓΓΑΡΙ

PÉENEE SAN SFOOGÁREE

HE DRINKS LIKE A SPONGE

🌀 HE DRINKS LIKE A FISH

ΘΑ ΚΑΨΟΥΜΕ ΤΟ ΠΕΛΕΚΟΥΔΙ

THA KÁPSOOME TO PELEKOOTHI

WE'LL BURN THE WOOD CHIP

🌀 WE'LL PAINT THE TOWN RED

🌀 WE LL HAVE A HELL OF A GOOD TIME

🌀 or at least IT'LL BE A LOT OF FUN

ΕΥΛΟΓΙΣΕ ΤΑ ΓΕΝΙΑ ΤΟΥ

ΕΝΛΟΎΓΕΕSE ΤΑ ΥΙΕΝΙΑ ΤΟΟ

HE BLESSED HIS BEARD

◎ EVERY MAN FOR HIMSELF
◎ HE TOOK CARE OF HIMSELF FIRST
◎ THE PRIEST BLESSES HIMSELF BEFORE
ANYONE ELSE.

ΕΜΕΙΣ ΜΠΡΙΚΙΑ ΚΟΛΛΑΜΕ;

ΕΜΕΈς ΒΡΕΈΚΙΑ ΚΟΛΛΆΜΕ;?

ARE WE WELDING COFFEE POTS?

◎ ARE WE HELPLESS?
◎ " " INCOMPETENT?
◎ " " STUPID?

A QUESTION BEGGING THE ANSWER.

27

ΑΛΛΑΞΕ ΤΡΟΠΑΡΙΟ

Állakse tropário

HE CHANGED HIS HYMN (CHANT)

🌀 HE CHANGED HIS TUNE

what else can I say?

ΣΕ ΠΟΥΛΑ ΚΑΙ Σ'ΑΓΟΡΑΖΕΙ

SE POOLÁ KE SAYORÁZEE

HE BUYS YOU AND SELLS YOU (or vice-versa)

◎ HE'S SMART AND SHREWD
◎ HE RUNS RINGS AROUND SOMEBODY

ΔΟΥΛΕΙΕΣ ΤΟΥ ΠΟΔΑΡΙΟΥ

THOOLIÉS TOO POTHARIOÓ

FOOT JOBS (LEG JOBS ?) *

◎ ODD JOBS
◎ A LESS THAN SERIOUS APPROACH
TO MAKING A LIVING.

* FOOT AND LEG IS THE SAME WORD IN MODERN GREEK
SO IS ARM & HAND. I DON'T KNOW WHY.

ΣAN TA BOYNA (n XIONIA)

SAN TA VOONÁ (or HIÓNIA)

LIKE THE MOUNTAINS (or SNOWS)

◎ LONG TIME - NO SEE

◎ YOU'RE QUITE A STRANGER

◎ HAVEN'T SEEN YOU IN AGES

31

TA EKANE POÏΔO

TA ÉKANE RÓΕETHO

HE MADE THEM POMEGRANATE

◎ HE MADE A MESS OF THINGS

◎ HE BUNGLED IT

* only one in the long list of expressions
  with the same meaning.

32

ΑΛΛΑΞΕ ΧΡΩΜΑ

Állakse hróma

HE/SHE/IT CHANGED COLOR

ⓖ HE WAS FLABBERGASTED

ⓖ HE WAS KNOCKED OFF HIS FEET

ΚΛΑΙΕΙ ΤΗΝ   ΜΟΙΡΑ ΤΟΥ
KLÉY TIN   MEÉRA TOO
HE IS CRYING HIS FATE

○ HE'S CRYING OVER HIS MISFORTUNES
○ HE'S DOWN THE DUMPS (DEPRESSED)

ΑΝΟΙΞΕ Η ΓΗ ΚΑΙ ΤΟΝ ΚΑΤΑΠΙΕ

ΑΝΕΕΚSΕ ΕΕ ΥΕΕ ΚΕ ΤΟΝ ΚΑΤΑΡΙΕ

THE EARTH OPENED UP AND SWALLOWED HIM

◎ HE VANISHED INTO THIN AIR

◎ HE DISAPPEARED

ΕΡΡΙΞΕ ΣΤΑΧΤΗ ΣΤΑ ΜΑΤΙΑ ΤΟΥ

ÉREEKSE STÁHTEE STA MÁTIA TOO

HE THREW ASHES IN HIS FACE

 HE PULLED THE WOOL OVER HIS EYES

TA MAΓAZIA ΣOY EIN' ANOIXTA

TA MAGAZIÁ SOO EEN'ANEEHTÁ

YOUR SHOPS ARE OPEN

◎ YOUR FLY'S OPEN !!

◎ HINT TO ZIP UP or
     BUTTON UP ONE'S FLY

ΣΗΚΩ-ΣΗΚΩ, ΚΑΤΣΕ-ΚΑΤΣΕ
SEÉKO-SEÉKO, KÁTSE-KÁTSE
SIT-SIT, GET UP GET UP
sorry the reverse

🌀 TO BOSS SOMEBODY AROUND
🌀 "SHE TELLS HIM TO JUMP AND
HE SAYS HOW HIGH"

ΧΑΦΤΕΙ ΜΥΓΕΣ

ΗΑΦΤΕΕ ΜΕΕΎΕΣ

HE/SHE 'S GULPING DOWN FLIES

◎ HE'S SITTING ON HIS HANDS
◎ HE'S WASTING TIME

ΤΟΝ ΠΗΡΕ ΣΤΟ ΨΙΛΟ ΓΑΖΙ

ΤΟΝ PEÉRE STO PSEELÓ YAZÉE

HE TOOK HIM TO A FINE STITCH

SHE
Ⓐ / HE WAS KIDDING HIM

Ⓑ HE WAS WORKING HIM OVER

Ⓒ HE WAS MAKING FUN OF HIM

ΠΑΙΖΕΙ ΤΟΝ ΠΑΠΑ

PÉZEE TON PAPÁ

HE'S PLAYING THE PRIEST

◎ HE'S DOUBLECROSSING US
(or them or somebody)

◎ HE'S CHEATING

ΕΒΓΑΛΕ ΤΟ ΛΑΡΥΓΓΙ ΤΟΥ

ÉVGALE TO LAREÉGEE TOO

HE TOOK HIS WINDPIPE OUT

◉ HE SHOUTED HIMSELF HOARSE

◎ HE YELLED AT THE TOP OF HIS VOICE

ΤΟΝ ΤΡΑΒΑΕΙ ΑΠ' ΤΗΝ ΜΥΤΗ

TON TRAVAEI APTIN MEÉTEE

SHE'S PULLING HIM BY THE NOSE

◎ SHE'S GOT HIM UNDER HER THUMB

ΑΠ' Τ' ΕΝΑ ΑΥΤΙ ΜΠΑΙΝΟΥΝ, ΑΠ' Τ' ΑΛΛΟ ΒΓΑΙΝΟΥΝ

ÁPTO ÉNA AFTI BÉNOON, ÁPTO ALLO VIÉNOON

THY GO IN ONE EAR, OUT THEY COME FROM THE OTHER

IN IT GOES ONE EAR, OUT THE OTHER

44

ΕΙΝΑΙ ΓΕΡΟ ΠΙΡΟΥΝΙ
ÉENE YERÓ PEEROÓNEE
HE IS A STRONG FORK

◎ HE'S A HEARTY EATER
◎ HE LOVES TO EAT

ΕΙΝΑΙ ΠΕΤΣΙ ΚΑΙ ΚΟΚΑΛΟ

ÉENE PETSÍ KE KÓKALO

HE IS SKIN AND BONE

HE IS SKIN AND BONES

ΔΕΝ ΒΛΕΠΕΙ   ΠΕΡΑ ΑΠΟ ΤΗΝ ΜΥΤΗ ΤΟΥ

ΤΗΕΝ VLÉPEE   PÉRA ΑΠΌ ΤΙΝ ΜΕΕΤΕΕ ΤΟΟ

HE CAN'T SEE   BEYOND HIS NOSE

Ⓖ HE'S NARROW MINDED
Ⓖ and he also LACKS FORESIGHT.

ΚΟΠΑΝΙΖΕΙ ΦΡΕΣΚΟ ΑΕΡΑ
KOPANÉEZEE FRÉSCO AERA
HE'S POUNDING FRESH AIR*

🌀 HE'S WASTING TIME, DOING NOTHING
🌀 HE'S LOAFING

*NOT IN ATHENS

48

ΤΟΥ ΧΑΜΟΓΕΛΑΣΕ Η ΤΥΧΗ

TOO HAMOYIÉLASE E TEÉHEE

HIS LUCK SMILED AT HIM

◎ HE GOT LUCKY

◎ HE LUCKED OUT (Amer.)

MOY KAΘHΣE ΣTO ΣTOMAXI

MOO CÁTHEESE STO STOMÁHI

HE SAT IN MY STOMACH

◉ I CAN'T STAND HIM

◉ I CAN'T PUT UP WITH HIM

NA ΣΕ ΒΡΑΣΩ

NA SE VRÁSSO

(Iought...) TO BOIL YOU

TO HELL WITH YOU

ΔΕΝ ΚΟΒΕΙ ΤΟ ΜΥΑΛΟ ΤΟΥ

THEN CO'VEE TO MEEALÓ TOO

HIS BRAIN DOESN'T CUT

- HE'S A BIT SLOW
- HE'S NOT TOO SHARP
- HE'S A MENTAL MIDGET

TA' ΠΕ ΧΑΡΤΙ ΚΑΙ ΚΑΛΑΜΑΡΙ

TÁPE HARTEÉ KE CALAMÁREE

HE TOLD IT PAPER AND INKPOT

◎ HE GAVE AN ACCOUNT IN EVERY DETAIL

◎ CHAPTER AND VERSE

TA KANE (E)ΠANO TOY
TÁKANE (E)PÁNO TOO
HE DID THEM ALL OVER HIMSELF

◎ HE DIRTIED HIS PANTS

◎ HE WAS SCARED STIFF

◎ HE WAS SCARED S---LESS

PIXNEI ΛΑΔI ΣΤΗ ΦΩΤΙΑ

REÉHNEE LÁTHI ΣTEE FOTIÁ

HE'S POURING OIL IN THE FIRE

Ⓞ HE'S ADDING FUEL TO THE FIRE

Ⓞ HE'S FANNING THE FLAMES

TOY BΓHKE ΑΠ'ΤΗΝ ΜΥΤΗ   (ΞΥΝΟ)

TOO VYEÉKE APTIN MEÉTEE (KSYNÓ) or (KSEENÓ)

IT CAME OUT OF HIS NOSE   (SOUR)

◎ SOMETHING TURNING BAD ON SOMEBODY,
   UNEXPECTEDLY.

◎ A BAD TURN OF EVENTS.

* ENTIRELY DIFFERENT MEANING THAN ΜΟΥ ΜΠΗΚΕ ΣΤΗΝ ΜΥΤΗ
HE/SHE ENTERED MY NOSE = HE/SHE BOTHERS ME. (VOLUME I)

56

ΚΥΝΗΓΑ ΤΟΝ ΠΟΔΟΓΥΡΟ

KEENEEYÁ TON POTHÓYEERO

HE'S CHASING THE SKIRT HEM

⊚ HE'S A SKIRT CHASER

⊚ HE'S A WOMANISER

ΔΕΝ ΣΗΚΩΝΕΙ ΔΕΥΤΕΡΗ ΚΟΥΒΕΝΤΑ
THEN SEEKÓNEE THÉFTERI KOOVÉNDA
HE DOES'T LIFT A SECOND WORD

◎ HE WILL HEAR NO OBJECTIONS
◎ HE TOLERATES NO ARGUMENTS
◎ IT'S CUT AND DRY

ΠΕΡΝΑ ΖΩΗ ΚΑΙ ΚΟΤΑ
PERNÁ ZOEÉ KE CÓTA
HE PASSES LIFE AND HEN

◎ HE LIVES IN CLOVER
◎ HE LIVES HIGH ON THE HOG
◎..THE LIFE OF RILEY (Amer.)

ΘΑ ΦΑΣ ΤΟ ΚΕΦΑΛΙ ΣΟΥ

THA FAS TO KEFÁLEE SOO

YOU'LL EAT YOUR HEAD

◉ YOU'RE RIDING FOR THE FALL

◉ YOU'RE DOING THE WRONG THING.

ΟΠΩΣ ΣΕ ΒΛΕΠΩ ΚΑΙ ΜΕ ΒΛΕΠΕΙΣ

ópos se VLÉPO ke meh VLÉPees

AS I SEE YOU AND YOU SEE ME

AS SURELY AS WE ARE STANDING HERE

TO CONVINCE SOMEBODY ABOOT ONE'S VERACITY

TON EΦEPE ΣTA NEPA TOY

TON ÉFERE STA NERÁ TOO

HE BROUGHT HIM OVER TO HIS WATERS

◉ HE WON HIM OVER

◉ HE BROUGHT HIM AROUND

ΓΕΛΑΣΕ ΚΑΙ ΤΟ ΠΑΡΔΑΛΟ ΚΑΤΣΙΚΙ

YÉLASE KE TO PARTHALÓ CATSÉEKEE

EVEN THE MOTLEY GOAT LAUGHED

EVERYBODY HAD A GOOD LAUGH

ΟΛΟΙ ΣΤΟ ΙΔΙΟ ΚΑΖΑΝΙ ΒΡΑΖΟΥΝ

ÓLEE STO EÉTHIO KAZÁNEE VRÁZOON

THEY ALL BOIL IN THE SAME CALDRON
(boiler)

◎ THEY ARE ALL IN THE SAME BOAT

◎ BIRDS OF A FEATHER....

64

ΔΕΝ ΣΗΚΩΝΕΙ ΑΣΤΕΙΑ

THEN SEEKÓNEE ASTEÉA

HE DOESN'T LIFT JOKES

◎ HE TOLERATES NO FOOLISHNESS

◎ HE'LL TAKE NO NONSENSE

ΛΟΓΑΡΙΑΖΕ ΧΩΡΙΣ ΤΟΝ ΞΕΝΟΔΟΧΟ

LOGÁRIAZE HOREÉS TON KSENOTHOHO

HE WAS COUNTING WITHOUT THE INNKEEPER

◎ HE WAS COUNTING HIS (EGGS) CHICKEN
BEFORE THEY WERE HATCHED

ΚΑΤΙ ΨΥΛΛΙΑΣΤΗΚΕ

KÁTEE PSEELIÁSTIKE

GOT COVERED BY FLEAS
(the best I could do)

◉ HE GOT A WHIFF OF SOMETHING.

◉ HE GOT SUSPICIOUS

◉ HE SMELLED A RAT

ΚΛΑΨΤΑ ΧΑΡΑΛΑΜΠΕ

KLÁPSTA HARALAMBE

CRY OVER THEM (C)HARALAMBUS

ΧΑΡΑΛΑΜΠΟΣ

◎ IT'S ALL OVER & DONE WITH

◎ NOTHING YOU CAN DO ABOUT IT

ΕΔΕΣΕ ΤΟΝ ΓΑΪΔΑΡΟ ΤΟΥ
ÉTHESE TON YÁITHARÓ TOO
HE TIED UP HIS DONKEY

⊚ HE'S SITTING PRETTY
⊚ HE'S PRETTY WELL SET UP
⊚ HE'S GOT NO WORIES

69

MOY ΚΑΘΕΣΕ ΣΤΟ ΣΒΕΡΚΟ

MOO KÁTHESE STO SVÉRKO

YOU'RE SITTING ON MY NAPE

◎ YOU'RE BUGGING ME

◎ YOU IRRITATE THE HELL OUT OF ME

ΕΦΑΓΕ ΤΟΝ ΚΟΣΜΟ

έφαγε τον cόsμο

HE/SHE ATE THE WORLD (OR PEOPLE)

⊚ HE LOOKED HIGH AND LOW

⊚ HE LEFT NO STONE UNTURNED

ΚΑΘΕ ΚΑΡΥΔΙΑΣ ΚΑΡΥΔΙ

Káthe careethiás careéthi

EVERY WALNUT TREE'S WALNUT

◎ EVERY MAN AND HIS DOG

◎ ALL THE WORLD AND HIS WIFE

◎ VARIOUS AND SUNDRY

ΤΟΝ ΠΕΡΑΣΕ ΑΠΟ ΨΙΛΟ ΚΟΣΚΙΝΟ

TON PÉRASE APÓ PSEELÓ COSKEENO

HE POT HIM THROUGH A FINE SIEVE

◎ HE SCREENED HIM THOROUGHLY

ΜΠΗΚΑΝ ΨΥΛΛΟΙ ΣΤ' ΑΥΤΙΑ ΜΟΥ

BEEKAN PSEÉLEE STAFTIÁ MOO

FLEAS GOT INTO MY EARS

◉ I SMELL A RAT

◉ I SUSPECT SOMETHING'S FISHY

ΕΙΝΑΙ ΑΠΟ ΜΕΓΑΛΟ ΤΖΑΚΙ

ÉENE APO MEGÁLO DZÁKEE

(HE/SHE) IS FROM A LARGE FIREPLACE

⊚ HE WAS BORN WITH
A SILVER SPOON IN HIS MOUTH

⊚ TO INDICATE ONE'S
IMPORTANCE

ΤΑ ΠΑΝΕ ΣΑΝ ΤΟΝ ΣΚΥΛΟ ΜΕ ΤΗΝ ΓΑΤΑ

TA PÁNE SAN TON SKEÉLO ME TEEN YÁTA

THEY GO LIKE THE DOG AND THE CAT

THEY FIGHT LIKE CATS AND DOGS

76

ΤΗΝ ΕΒΑΨΕ

ΤΕΕΝ ΕVΑPSΕ

HE PAINTED HER

◉ HE'S IN A PICKLE
◉ HE'S IN A FIX
◉ or more deci

HE'S BANKRUPT

ΔΕΝ ΠΗΡΑ ΜΥΡΩΔΙΑ

THEN PEÉRA MEEROTHIÁ

I RECEIVED NO SMELL

◎ I HAD NO IDEA, NO HINT, NO CLUE

◎ I DIDN'T SUSPECT ANYTHING

ΤΟΥ ΄ΔΩΣΕ ΤΑ ΠΑΠΟΥΤΣΙΑ ΣΤΟ ΧΕΡΙ

TOOTHOSE TA PAPOOTSIA STO HÉREE

SHE/HE GAVE HIM THE SHOES IN HIS HAND

◎ HE WAS TOLD TO LEAVE IN NO UNCERTAIN WORDS

◎ HE/SHE FIRED HIM

◎ HE GOT THE BOOT

◎ HE WAS SACKED

ΕΜΕΙΝΕ ΣΤΑ ΚΡΥΑ ΤΟΥ ΛΟΥΤΡΟΥ

ÉMEENE STA KREÉA TOO LOOTROÓ

HE WAS LEFT IN THE COLD OF THE BATH

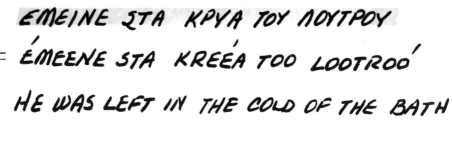

◉ HE WAS LEFT IN THE LURCH

◉ HE WAS LEFT OUT IN THE COLD

KANAME MAYPA MATIA NA ΣΕ ΔOYME
KÁNAME MÁVRA MÁTIA NA SE THOÓME
WE MADE BLACK EYES TO SEE YOU

◎ LONG TIME - NO SEE (amer.)
◎ IT'S BEEN A LONG TIME

ΦΑΕ ΤΗΝ ΓΛΩΣΣΑ ΣΟΥ

FÁE TEEN GLÓSSA SOO

EAT YOUR TONGUE

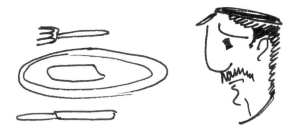

BITE YOUR TONGUE

TA'ΧΕΙ   ΤΕΤΡΑΚΟΣΙΑ

ΤΆΗΕΕ   ΤΕΤΡΑΚΌΣΙΑ

HE HAS THEM (400) FOUR HUNDRED   400
                                   ;?

◎ HE IS AS SHARP AS A RAZOR

◎ HE IS A SMART FELLOW

ΦΟΥΣΚΩΣΑΝ ΤΑ ΜΥΑΛΑ ΤΟΥ

FOOSKOSAN TA MIALÁ 'TOO

HIS BRAINS PUFFED OUT

HE' GROWN TOO BIG FOR HIS BOOTS
(or BRITCHES)

KANEI TON ΨΟΦΙΟ ΚΟΡΙΟ

KÁNEE TON PSÓFIO KORIÓ

HE'S PRETENDING TO BE A DEAD BED BUG

◎ HE'S PLAYING POSSUM

ΔEN TON XΩNEYΩ
THEN TON HONEVO
I DON'T DIGEST HIM

- I CAN'T STAND HIM
- I CAN'T PUT UP WITH HIM
- I CAN'T STOMACH HIM

KOMMENOΣ KAI PAMMENOΣ

COMÉNOS KE RAMÉNOS

HE IS CUT AND STITCHED

- HE'S CUT OUT FOR ....
- HE'S TAILOR MADE FOR A JOB

ΆΡΕΣ, ΜΑΡΕΣ, ΚΟΥΚΟΥΝΑΡΕΣ
ÁRES, MÁRES, KOOKOONÁRES
?   ?   PINE CONES

A GREEK.... ALLITERATION OR RHYME
MEANING :
◎ BALDERDASH
◎ HOG-WASH
◎ BLAH-BLAH
◎ TALKING THROUGH ONE'S HAT

ΘΑ ΣΕ ΦΑΩ ΖΩΝΤΑΝΟ

THA SE FÁO ZONDANÓ

I "LL EAT YOU ALIVE

Ⓣ I "LL SKIN YOU ALIVE

MOY ANAΨAN TA ΛAMΠAKIA

MOO ÁNAPSAN TA LAMBÁKIA

MY LITTLE LIGHTS WENT ON

◎ I SAW RED

◉ I BLEW MY TOP

TPABAEI TON ΔIAOΛO TOY

TRAVÁEE TON THIAOLÓ TOO

HE'S PULLING HIS DEVIL

◎ HE'S HAVING A DEVIL OF A TIME
◎ HE'S REALLY SUFFERING

ΜΠΟΡΑ ΕΙΝΑΙ, ΘΑ ΠΕΡΑΣΕΙ
BÓRA EÉNE, THA PERÁSEE

IT'S ONLY A RAIN SHOWER, IT"LL PASS

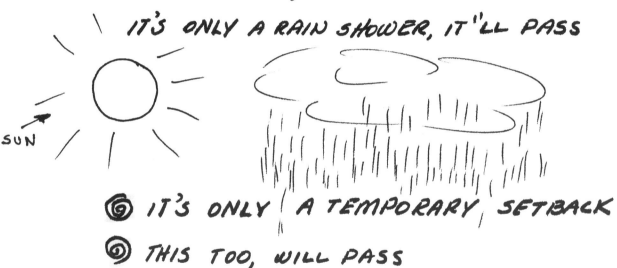

SUN

◎ IT'S ONLY A TEMPORARY SETBACK

◎ THIS TOO, WILL PASS

ΔΕΝ ΞΕΡΕΙ ΤΑ DYO KAKA ΤΗΣ ΜΟΙΡΑΣ ΤΟΥ

THEN KSÉREE TA THIÓ KAKÁ TIS MEÉPHS TOO

HE DOESN'T KNOW THE TWO BADS OF HIS FATE

B   A

◎ HE DOESN'T KNOW A FROM B
◎ HE DOESN'T KNOW IF HE'S COMING
                    OR GOING.

ÉKANE ①TEPA

ÉKANE FTERÁ

HE/SHE/IT GREW WINGS

◎ HE VANISHED INTO THIN AIR

◎ HE/SHE/IT DISAPPEARED

(INEXPLICABLY)

94

ΓΛΥΤΩΣΕ ΑΠ' ΤΟΥ ΧΑΡΟΥ ΤΑ ΔΟΝΤΙΑ

(GL) YLEÉTOSE APTOÓ HÁROO TA THONDIA

HE ESCAPED FROM THE GRIM REAPER'S TEETH

HE WAS SAVED BY THE SKIN OF HIS TEETH

ΞΕΧΕΙΛΙΣΕ ΤΟ ΠΟΤΗΡΙ

KSEHEÉLEESE TO POTÉEREE

THE GLASS RUNETH OVER

 ENOUGH IS ENOUGH

ME TO ΜΑΛΑΚΟ

ME TO MALAKÓ

WITH THE SOFT

 GO EASY

ΠΗΡΕ ΔΡΟΜΟ

PEÉRE THROMO

HE TOOK THE ROAD

◎ HE TOOK OFF LIKE A BAT OUT OF HELL

◎ HE MADE TRACKS

ΒΡΑΣΕ ΡΥΖΙ
VRÁSE REÉZEE
BOIL RICE

◎ A STATEMENT OF RESIGNATION

◎ OH WELL, WHAT CAN YOU DO?

PROVERBS

and a few proverbs just for fun!

ΜΙΑ ΣΤΟ ΚΑΡΦΙ ΚΑΙ ΜΙΑ ΣΤΟ ΠΕΤΑΛΟ

MIÁ STO CARFÉE KE MIÁ STO PÉTALO

ONCE ON THE NAIL AND ONCE ON THE HORSESHOE

- BLOW HOT AND COLD
- UP ONE MINUTE DOWN THE NEXT
- UNPREDICTABLE - UNRELIABLE

ΑΝ ΕΙΣΑΙ ΚΑΙ ΠΑΠΑΣ ΜΕ ΤΗΝ ΑΡΑΔΑ ΣΟΥ ΘΑ ΠΑΣ

AN EÉSE KE PAPÁS ME TIN ARÁTHA SOO THA PÁS

EVEN IF YOU ARE A PRIEST YOU WAIT YOUR TURN

◎ FIRST COME, FIRST SERVED
◎ LATE COME, LATE SERVED.

A VERY HANDY AND EASY (RHYMING) PHRASE TO USE
WHEN SOMEBODY IS TRYING TO OVERTAKE YOU IN A LINE (QUEUE)
A VERY FREQUENTLY OCCURING PHENOMENON IN GREECE

Η ΤΡΕΛΑ ΔΕΝ ΠΑΕΙ ΣΤΑ ΒΟΥΝΑ

EE TRÉLA THEN PÁEE STA VOONÁ

INSANITY GOES NOT IN THE MOUNTAINS

◎ HE IS CRAZY
◎ HE IS A RAVING LUNATIC

MAΘHMENA TA BOYNA AΠO TA XIONIA

MATHEEMÉNA TA VOONÁ ÁPTA HIÓNIA

THE MOUNTAINS ARE USED TO SNOW

① NO STRANGER TO ADVERSITY

ΟΠΟΥ ΛΑΛΟΥΝ ΠΟΛΛΟΙ ΚΟΚΟΡΟΙ ΑΡΓΕΙ ΝΑ ΞΗΜΕΡΩΣΕΙ
ópoo laloón pollée kokóree aryeé na ksimerósee

WHERE TOO MANY ROOSTERS CROW, IT TAKES LONGER
FOR DAWN TO COME.

(9) TOO MANY COOKS SPOIL THE BROTH
(9) TOO MANY CHIEFS AND NOT ENOUGH INDIANS.
(A PERMANENT STATE OF AFFAIRS IN GREECE)

ΚΑΛΙΟ ΓΑΪΔΟΥΡΟΔΕΝΕ ΠΑΡΑ ΓΑΙΔΟΥΡΟΓΥΡΕΥΕ

KALIO YAITHOORÓTHENE PARÁ YAITHODRO YEÉREVE

BETTER TIE YOUR DONKEY DOWN RATHER THAN RUN AFTER IT.

PREVENTION IS BETTER THAN CURE

ΟΠΟΙΟΣ ΒΙΑΖΕΤΑΙ ΣΚΟΝΤΑΦΤΗ

όPIOS VIÁZETE SKONDAFTEE

WHOEVER IS IN A HURRY STUMBLES

LOOK BEFORE YOU LEAP

ΣΤΟΥ ΚΟΥΦΟΥ ΤΗΝ ΠΟΡΤΑ ΟΣΟ ΘΕΛΕΙΣ ΒΡΟΝΤΑ

stoo coofoó tin pórta oso thélis vrónda

YOU CAN KNOCK ALL YOU WANT ON A DEAF MAN'S DOOR.

DON'T WASTE YOUR BREATH

ΑΚΟΜΑ ΔΕΝ ΤΟΝ ΕΙΔΑΜΕ, ΓΙΑΝΝΗ ΤΟΝ ΕΒΓΑΛΑΜΕ

ACÓMA THEN TON EÉTHAME, YIÁNEE TON EV·YÁLAME

WE HAVEN'T SEEN HIM YET   WE NAMED HIM JOHN

JOHN

⑨ DON'T COUNT YOUR CHICKENS
   BEFORE THEY HATCH.

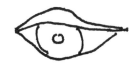 

ΜΑΤΙΑ ΠΟΥ ΔΕΝ ΒΛΕΠΟΝΤΑΙ
        ΓΡΗΓΟΡΑ ΛΗΣΜΟΝΙΟΥΝΤΑΙ

MÁTIA POO THEN VLÉPONDE
        GREÉYORA LEESMÓNIOONDE

EYES THAT DON'T SEE EACHOTHER
        ARE QUICKLY FORGOTTEN

⑥ OUT OF SIGHT - OUT OF MIND.

112

HURRAH !!

◎ a bonus ◎

◎ MORE PEJORATIVES

* useful

** very useful, but risky

*** et. al. (very-very useful but
     very-very risky

**** downright dangerous.

⊚ SOME CULTURAL, LINGUISTIC NOTATIONS & WARNINGS.

ΕΙΣΑΙ (EÉSE) = YOU ARE
ΕΙΝΑΙ (EÉNE) = HE/SHE/IT IS

Sometimes it is expedient to use the third person, quietly as an aside, loudly enough to be heard, but leaving you enough room to diplomatically claim you were referring to someone else!

ΤΟΥ ΣΤΡΙΨΕ Η ΒΙΔΑ *

ΤΟΟ STREEPSE EE VEETHA

HIS SCREW WAS TURNED

© HE'S GOT A SCREW LOOSE

© HE'S OFF HIS ROCKER

ΣΟΥ ΣΤΡΙΨΕ.. - SOO STREEPSE.... YOU'VE GOT....

EIΣAI   KAΘAPMA   * * *

EÉSE   KÁTHARMA

YOU ARE A SCOUNDREL

ALSO
◎   ... A VILLAIN
◎   A RASCAL
◎   A SCUM
        NOT TO MENTION ◎ A HEEL and
                    ◎ A CREEP

**

EΙΣΑΙ
(EINAI)
- A-ΚΕΦΑΛΑΣ
- B-ΜΠΟΥΜΠΟΥΝΑΣ
- C-ΜΠΟΥΖΟΥΚΟΚΕΦΑΛΟΣ

EÉSE
(EENE)
- A-KEFÁLAS
- B-BOOBOÓNAS
- C-BOOZOOKOKÉFALOS

YOU ARE
(HE/SHE/IT) IS
- A- BIG HEADED
- B- THICK SKULLED
- C- BOUZOUKI SKULLED

YOU ARE
(HE/SHE/IT IS)
- a- JACKASS b-numskull c-clod
- d- dope   e- fathead f-blockhead
- g- pigheaded, h-an idiot

118

ΕΙΝΑΙ ΒΛΑΚΑΣ ΜΕ (a) ΠΕΡΙΚΕΦΑΛΑΙΑ
(b) ΠΑΤΕΝΤΑ , ***

ΕΕΝΑΙ VLÁKAS MEH (a) PERIKEFALÉA
(b) PATÉNDA

HE IS AN IDIOT WITH (a) HELMET
(b) PATENT

◎ HE IS AN UNMITIGATED IDIOT

◎ HE IS UTTERLY STUPID
AND BESIDES THAT, ALSO AN ASS

YOU MAY CHANGE THIS INTO A
PEJORATIVE, SIMPLY BY SUBSTITUTING
ΕΙΣΑΙ - ÉESE for ΕΙΝΑΙ - ÉENE
MEANING "YOU-ARE...."

ΕΙΣΑΙ   ΚΟΠΑΝΟΣ   ****

ΕέSE   CÓPANOS

YOU ARE A MALLET (PESTLE)

⊚ YOU ARE (a) A NUMBSKULL
            (b) A NITWIT
            (c) A TWIT
            (d) A JERK
            (e) ALL OF THE ABOVE

ΕΙΣΑΙ ΜΠΟΥΡΔΑΣ **
ÉÉSE BOURTHAS
YOU SPEAK NONSENSE

NONSENSE
BOURTHES

◉ YOU ARE A BIG MOUTH
◉ YOU ARE A LOUD MOUTH.

ΕΙΣΑΙ   ΜΟΥΡΛΟΣ   ***
EÉSE   MOORLÓS
YOU ARE   A LUNATIC

@ YOU ARE DEMENTED
@ YOU ARE MENTALLY DERANGED
@ YOU ARE A RAVING LUNATIC
@ YOU ARE NUTS
@ YOU ARE CRAZY

REMEMBER   EÉNE = HE/SHE IS

ΤΗΝ ΨΩΝΙΣΕ	ΕΙΝΑΙ ΨΩΝΙΟ *
TIN PSÓNEESE	EÉNE PSÓNIO
HE/SHE BOUGHT HER	HE/SHE IS A PURCHASE

◎ HE/SHE'S GONE CRAZY -

◎ HE/SHE'S A RAVING LUNATIC

ΘΑ ΣΟΥ ΣΠΑΣΩ ΤΑ ΜΟΥΤΡΑ ***

THA sou SPÁSO TA MOÚTRA

I WILL BREAK YOUR FACE

🌀 THE EQUIVALENT OF THE VERY EXPRESSIVE AND SENSITIVE ITALIAN PHRASE "I AMA GONNA BREAKA YOUR FACE"

** WARNING. A RATHER DIRECT STATEMENT!!
SOME GREEKS MAY TAKE IT AS A THREAT.
USE ONLY WHEN THEY ARE 1/3 OF YOUR SIZE

ΒΓΑΛΕ ΤΟΝ ΣΚΑΣΜΟ! ****
Vgále ton skasmó!
TAKE OUT THE SUFFOCATION !!

◎ SHUT YOUR TRAP!
◎ HOLD YOUR TONGUE
◎ SHUT UP

ΝΑ ΠΑΣ ΚΑΙ ΝΑ ΜΗ ΓΥΡΙΣΕΙΣ   ***

ΝΑ PAS KE NA MEE YEEREÉSEES

GO AND DON'T COME BACK

⊚ GET LOST
⊚ SCRAM
⊚ GOOD RIDDANCE
⊚ GO TO HELL
⊚ BEAT IT

WHAT OTHERS SAID

The huge success of VOLUME I indicates that the intellectual level of our population has diminished to a dangerously low level. **THE CRITIC**

Those who can, do. Those who can't... write **TA PALIA**

No, Not again. For Pete's sake why didn't he keep up his kite flying, he was doing so well with it **HIS SISTER VERNA**

Vernon who?
His father **VAS**

What can we say?
HIS THREE SONS - IN UNISON

I told him he should take an art class, even at his age. **NATASHULA**

About Mr. Elliott

He still doesn't look like that
and he still would like to.

It is certain by now that Vernon does not take himself too seriously, although he must have at sometime. It just does not become a college graduate to take up kite flying.

At any rate he has become a rather withdrawn individual in search of a country, since he lost both of them. He has been travelling interminably looking for them. The disease, the "Ulysses complex" has severely limited his ability to draw, not to mention that he rarely takes care of his teddy bear any longer.

He is still reasonably likeable, it obtrose at times, can't spell too well but has vowed Never-ever again to postpone JOY. He remains uncommited as to whether his name is Vernon Elliott or Elliott Vernon Perhaps he does not know for sure himself.

At any rate, to make a short story long, Vernon is a semi-well travelled person, who after his divorce, first he started to laugh (or cry?) uncontrollably out of sheer gratitude and then refused to take ANYTHING seriously

He was semi-educated in Greece and later in the U.S.A. and for almost twenty years he led a semi-normal existence doing semi-normal things. Having preference for the semi-abnormal however, he has spent the last 12 years or so doing practically nothing and then resting afterwards.

Being constantly intoxicated from the well from within him, on certain quasi-creative outbursts he composes semi-satirical little books like this one, the 4th or maybe 5th in the series — just for the fun of it as well as for profit which allows him to buy premium quality toothpaste for a whole year.

Besides doing nothing, he also enjoys chocholate, sailing

eating, kite flying, samba dancing, painting, pottery music, listening and composing, fixing things that don't need fixing and unfixing things that do, and a few other things which are unprintable and have nothing to do with solving crossword puzzles.

He definately does not like shopping.

Mr Elliott loves Greece passionately and desperately wishes he could harbor similar sentiments about some of her inhabitants, mostly the politicians and those who defile the most beautiful land in the whole planet.

BY THE SAME AUTHOR

1. GREEK: A FRACTURED LEXICON VOLUME I
   Over 300 idioms, phrases, pejoratives and sounds, absolutely
   necessary to communicate in Greek or even to amuse yourself.

2. GREEK: A FRACTURED LEXICON VOLUME II
   125 or so more of the above.

3. A VISITOR'S GUIDE TO MODERN GREEK BEHAVIOR AND HABITS
   A tongue-in-cheek approach to the culture shock.

4. A VISITOR'S GUIDE TO GREEK DRIVING? AND OTHER OXYMORA
AND PARADOXA
   1001 things a visitor needs to know, or just to laugh.

5. GREECE WITHOUT TEARS
   A guide for those who prefer the non-touristy approach to
   travel.

Mr Elliottt has authored several other works which, however, no publisher has
dared as yet to accept.

ORDER FORM

PLEASE MAIL TO ....
                          name

AT ....
                          address

....
city   state   zip

	How many	times ea.	total
GREEK-A FRACTURED LEXICON I	....	....	....
GREEK-A FRACTURED LEXICON II	....	....	....
GREEK BEHAVIOR & HABITS	....	....	....
GREEK DRIVING	....	....	....
GREECE WITHOUT TEARS	....	....	....

POSTAGE & HANDLING $ 2.50 FIRST + $ .50 each additional

VISA-MC-AMEX-CHECK-M.OM.   ....
                                          credit card, number

SPECIAL WHOLESALE PRICES AVAILABLE FOR FUND RAISERS,
BOOK STORES, TRAVEL AGENCIES E.T.C.

mail to:

REGENT
2950 North U.S. 41
Naples, Florida
33940

tel. (813) 263-6622